OKAVANGO

AN AFRICAN PARADISE

To my wife, Sharna.

OKAVANGO

AN AFRICAN PARADISE

Photography & text by

DARYL BALFOUR

STRUIK

Struik Publishers
(a member of the Struik Group (Pty) Ltd)
Struik House
Oswald Pirow Street
Foreshore
Cape Town
8001

Reg. No.: 63/00203/07

First published 1990

Text © Daryl Balfour
Photographs © Daryl Balfour, except p19 LEFT © Philip Huebsch.

Design by Petal Palmer
Typesetting by McManus Bros (Pty) Ltd, Cape Town
Reproduction by Unifoto (Pty) Ltd, Cape Town
Printed and bound by National Book Printers, Goodwood

ISBN 0 86977 712 2

FRONTISPIECE *The sitatunga is one of the world's rarer animals. It is a member of the kudu family and the most aquatic of all antelope, with features specially developed for the marshy habitat which it prefers.*

PREVIOUS PAGE *The Cape buffalo, regarded by many to be Africa's most dangerous animal, is one of the most numerous of the Okavango's large game species.*

OPPOSITE *The meandering 100- kilometre journey through the Panhandle is the last time the Okavango flows as a single river, for hereafter it spills over onto the shifting sands of the Kalahari and fans out to form the Okavango Delta, Africa's last great wilderness.*

PAGE 7 *A lioness peers inquisitively at the camera from beneath an umbrella of mopane scrub.*

PAGES 8-9 *First discovered by naturalist, explorer and artist Captain William Cornwallis Harris in 1838, the sable antelope is one of the most magnificent and striking of all the antelope. Both male and female carry sweeping, curved horns, and while the adult male is almost a pure black, the females and young sable are chestnut in colour.*

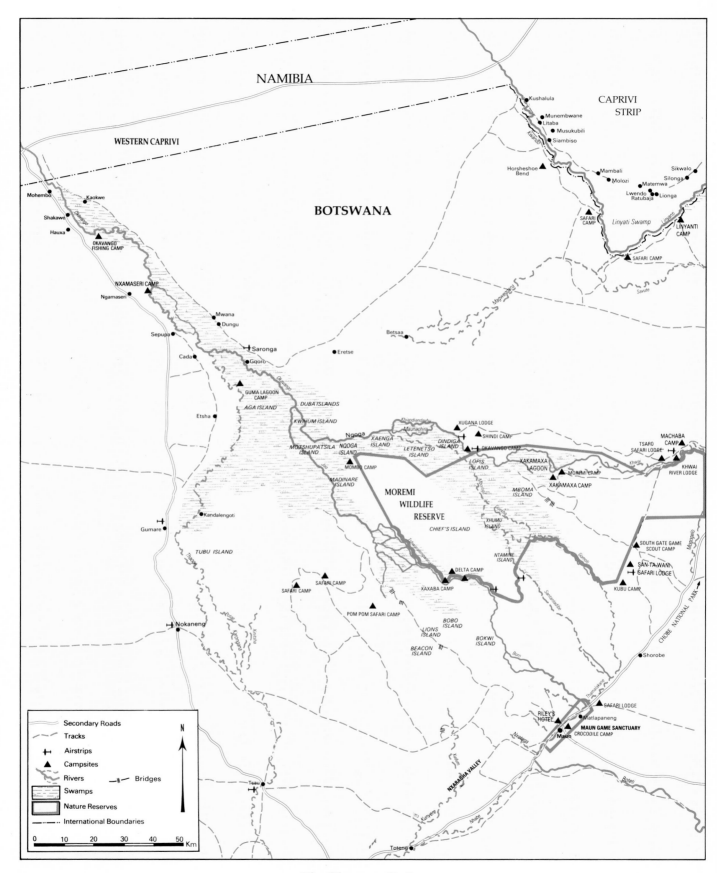

NAMIBIA

WESTERN CAPRIVI

CAPRIVI
STRIP

BOTSWANA

● Kushalula
● Munembwane
● Litaba
● Musukubili
● Siambiso

Horsheshoe
Bend

● Mambali
● Molozi

● Sikwalo
● Silonga
● Matemwa

Lwendo
Ratubaja ● Lionga

SAFARI
CAMP

Linyati Swamp

LINYANTI
CAMP

▲ SAFARI CAMP

● Mohembo
● Kaokwe

● Shakawe
● Hauxa

OKAVANGO
FISHING CAMP

NXAMASERI CAMP

● Ngamaseri

● Mwana
● Dungu

● Sepupa

● Cada
Saronga
● Gqoro

GUMA LAGOON
CAMP

AGA ISLAND

● Etsha

DUBA ISLANDS

KWIHUM ISLAND

● Betsaa

● Eretse

Khandiandadu
Maunachira

XUGANA LODGE
SHINDI CAMP

MACHABA
CAMP

TSARO
SAFARI LODGE

Nqoga

XAENGA
ISLAND

MOTSHUPATSILA
ISLAND

NQOGA
ISLAND

LETENETSO
ISLAND

DINDIGA
ISLAND
OKAVANGO CAMP

LOPIS
ISLAND

XAKAMAXA
LAGOON

MOREMI CAMP

KHWAI
RIVER LODGE

MOMBO CAMP

MADINARE
ISLAND

MOREMI
WILDLIFE
RESERVE

MBOMA
ISLAND

XAKAMAXA CAMP

● Kandalengoti

CHIEF'S ISLAND

XHUMU
ISLAND

SOUTH GATE GAME
SCOUT CAMP

Gumare

TUBU ISLAND

DELTA CAMP

NTAMINE
ISLAND

SAN-TA-WAN
SAFARI LODGE

SAFARI CAMP

SAFARI CAMP

XAXABA CAMP

KUBU CAMP

POM POM SAFARI CAMP

● Nokaneng

LIONS
ISLAND

BOBO
ISLAND

BOKWI
ISLAND

● Shorobe

BEACON
ISLAND

CHOBE NATIONAL PARK

SAFARI LODGE

RILEY'S
HOTEL

● Matlapaneng

MAUN GAME SANCTUARY
CROCODILE CAMP

Maun

NXARAGHA VALLEY

● Tsau

● Toteng

	Secondary Roads
	Tracks
	Airstrips
▲	Campsites
	Rivers — Bridges
	Swamps
	Nature Reserves
	International Boundaries

N

0   10   20   30   40   50
Km

The Okavango Delta

INTRODUCTION

TOP *Maun is the administrative capital of the Ngamiland district, and the gateway to the Okavango.*

ABOVE *The best way to get a true overview of the Okavango Delta is from the air.*

AFRICA'S LAST GREAT unspoiled wilderness, the Okavango Delta, is situated in the northern reaches of Botswana, one of the least densely populated nations on earth. It is an unexpected oasis, a glittering expanse of crystal-clear waterways, lush green papyrus and fertile floodplains, surrounded on all sides by arid semi-desert and Kalahari sandveld.

Rising on the Benguela Plateau in the highlands of central Angola is the Okavango, southern Africa's third largest river, and the largest in the world that does not flow into the sea. It begins life as two tributaries, the Cuito and Cubango, which, fed by rainwater runoff, rush headlong southeastwards – inland across the southern Angolan savanna. These two rivers soon join together, to ultimately form the mighty Okavango, flowing along Namibia's northern border before crossing the Caprivi Strip and tumbling over the Popa Falls into northwestern Botswana near the village of Mohembo.

Here the river slows its pace and begins its meandering, 100-kilometre journey through the Panhandle. This narrow strip of wetland at the northern extremity of the Okavango Delta is formed as the river reaches the Gumare Fault and is channelled by this southernmost extension of the Great Rift Valley of East Africa.

In the Panhandle, the Okavango is a mighty river, more than a kilometre wide in places. Winding its way southwards, it flows alternately through acres of luxuriant papyrus floating in its own root mass or beneath towering wild fig and ebony trees offering shade on the high river banks.

In these upper reaches the river, with its strong flow and deep waters, is home to the predatory tigerfish, a powerful fighter which provides some of the best angling in the Okavango, attracting sport fishermen from around the world. Delectable river bream can also be found, while each year the annual barbel (catfish) run churns the water in a frenzy as tens of thousands of these fish congregate here.

Myriad birds make their nests in the reeds and trees flanking the river, while the broad, shallow sandbars provide a habitat for the unique African skimmer, a bird which feeds by flying low over the water with the blade-like tip of its lower jaw cleaving the surface, snapping closed on any small fish with which it comes into contact. Tiny jewel-like malachite kingfishers add a splash of colour as they perch quietly over a still backwater, waiting to swoop on any unwary prey that ventures too close to the surface.

This too, is where the biggest crocodiles in the Okavango are to be found, with sightings of four- and five-metre-long monsters not uncommon. More than a hundred crocodile nesting sites have been identified in the Panhandle. Crocodiles lay between 20 and 90 eggs in nests dug near the river bank, and these are then incubated by the sun-warmed sand for about three months. When the young are due to hatch they start calling from the nest, a high-pitched squeaking sound that can be heard by the human ear as much as two metres away. The mother, who has remained nearby all this time, goes to the nest and excavates her newly hatched young, which she then gently carries to the water in her mouth. Baby crocodiles are very vulnerable at this stage, and despite staying near the mother, very few survive to maturity in the wild.

Along the banks are the villages of the river people, the Mbukushu, who settled in this area early last century after being displaced by warlike tribes in central Africa. Legendary rainmakers, the Mbukushu are traditionally agriculturalists; although they do make the *mokoro*, a dug-out canoe which they propel by use of a pole, their fishing and hunting exploits are of secondary importance to them.

The Okavango slows its pace as it meanders further down the Panhandle, becoming shallower as its load of silt and sediment is deposited. It has been claimed that the river is slowly choking in its own sediment, with as much as 600 000 tons of silt deposited yearly.

In these lower reaches papyrus becomes the dominant riverside vegetation, floating like huge green rafts on either side of the river. This is the chosen domain of the sitatunga, an aquatic antelope that has evolved as a specialist swamp dweller. It has elongated and widely splayed hooves – enabling it to traverse marshy peat bogs and matted reed beds without sinking through the surface – and a thick, water-repellent coat.

The sitatunga is the only large mammal that lives in and eats papyrus, a plant unpalatable to most creatures. The male weighs up to 100 kilograms, and carries a handsome set of spiral horns that grow to about 75 centimetres. It is when alarmed or injured that this animal displays its most remarkable characteristic, for then it will plunge headlong into the water in an attempt to reach safety – in extreme cases submerging completely, with just its nostrils above the surface.

The journey through the Panhandle is the last time the Okavango flows as a single river by that name, for hereafter it fans out to become the Okavango Delta, a 16 000-square-kilometre wilderness of sparkling waterways and enchanted islands.

Although much of the early history of the Okavango is still subject to considerable scientific debate, there is common consensus that a vast inland sea or super-lake once covered what are today the dry salt flats of the Makgadikgadi Pans, to the south of the Okavango. The size of the super-lake, today referred to as Lake Makgadikgadi, has been estimated at between 30 000 and 80 000 square kilometres and 100 metres deep. While theories differ as to whether the Okavango itself was part of the lake, it is generally believed that the Delta did not exist, and that rather the Okavango River, along with the Chobe and Zambezi rivers, flowed into the lake.

The whole of northern Botswana is geologically unstable and the earth's crust is subject to considerable stress and movement. There are several major fault lines in the area, and these, combined with a gradual tilting and uplifting of the earth's surface, probably caused the diversion of both the Chobe and Zambezi rivers, thereby causing the draining and drying up of Lake Makgadikgadi. The tilting of the earth's surface also caused the creation of a huge trough which absorbed the flow of the Okavango. In time this trough filled with silt, windswept sand and organic debris, to become the Okavango Delta.

Although widely referred to as 'the swamps', this term could hardly be a more misleading one for the Delta, for the water is not the warm, muddy liquid one usually associates with swamplands, but clear and cool –

TOP *During the flood season, four-wheel-drive vehicles are the only way to get around.*

ABOVE *Tucked away on isolated islands throughout the Delta are many cosy safari camps such as this one on Shindi Island.*

TOP *Foot safaris allow people the opportunity to encounter wildlife at close quarters, while being supervised by experienced, armed guides.*

ABOVE *The tigerfish is regarded as one of the premier freshwater fighting fishes in the world.*

thousands of glittering channels, huge blue oxbow lakes and lagoons filled with some of the purest water in Africa, if not the world. This is an enchanted wilderness, the last oasis in an Africa rapidly succumbing to the pressures of 20th century development, rampant population growth, and environmental sabotage.

Home to an incredible variety of fish, birds, mammals and insects, this is where the real magic of the Okavango can be experienced: exploring secret waterways and hidden channels; marvelling at densely wooded islands rich in birdlife; and wondering at the fertile floodplains teeming with a variety of wild game. Waterlilies in many hues choke the channels, and in places the papyrus knits overhead to block out the sky. Occasionally, the channels widen and form open stretches of water, where hippo may surface with a startling snort, and fix you with a curious stare. Here, you may also sight the delicate pygmy goose feeding on lily seeds around the lagoon perimeter, and the skillfully woven nests of weaver birds hanging precariously from the tips of thin branches over the edge of the water.

The islands are perhaps the Okavango's greatest feature: it is estimated there are more than 50 000 of them, some little more than termite mounds rising above the surrounding waters. Others may be large enough to support permanent herds of game, sprawling tourist camps and centuries-old trees and forests. The largest of them all, Chief's Island, is part of the Moremi Game Reserve and extends more than 50 kilometres from top to bottom and as much as 20 kilometres across. This is the only major landmass in the heart of the Okavango waterways.

The larger islands are shady havens amid the relentless papyrus swamps, where delicate wild date palms are scattered among the thorny acacias, towering wild ebony, or *mokuchumo*, and sausage trees. Here you may find the Pel's fishing owl, asleep in the deepest shade. At night it ventures to its favourite perch above an open stretch of water, from where it searches for food. Once the owl has seen its prey, it plummets feet first into the water, sometimes submerging entirely in its determination to seize a fish. On surfacing, it flies to a nearby tree limb where it kills and consumes the fish, often returning to the same spot time after time and thereby leaving a tell-tale indication to sharp-eyed observers – a pile of fish scales and other remains beneath a shady tree often denotes the existence of a Pel's owl nearby.

The Okavango boasts about 400 different species of birds, not perhaps all as interesting as the Pel's fishing owl, but certainly a wonderful challenge to the enthusiastic birdwatcher. It is the Okavango Delta's many islands that provide the best birdwatching, for out in the waterways and among the papyrus reeds dwell only a limited number of swamp specialists...and they are difficult to see.

Among the most spectacular of the birds are the raptors, or birds of prey, and of these the majestic fish eagle undoubtedly is the most magnificent. Its piercing cry, often a breeding pair in duet, is one of the most evocative sounds of Africa and can be heard welcoming the dawn throughout the Okavango. There can be few sights more thrilling than that of this magnificent bird swooping to snatch a fish from near the surface of the delta's waterways.

Other birds of prey that may be seen include the mighty martial eagle, both the brown and black-breasted snake eagles, as well as that incredible aviator, the bateleur – one of the most colourful of all eagles – and four of the vulture species.

But it is the small birds that provide the most colour, and for many, the most interest. Spectacular nesting colonies of carmine bee-eaters can be found either in river banks, or, in certain areas (such as Shindi Island and near the Four Rivers bushman village), in flat, sandy ground. On early

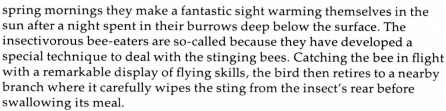

spring mornings they make a fantastic sight warming themselves in the
sun after a night spent in their burrows deep below the surface. The
insectivorous bee-eaters are so-called because they have developed a
special technique to deal with the stinging bees. Catching the bee in flight
with a remarkable display of flying skills, the bird then retires to a nearby
branch where it carefully wipes the sting from the insect's rear before
swallowing its meal.

The lilac-breasted roller, surely one of the most magnificent birds in
creation, can be seen in many parts of the Delta. Stately wattled cranes,
striding regally across the floodplains, are a seriously endangered species
that have found a refuge here, while ducks and geese mingle freely with
numerous other waterbirds, storks and herons. Should you be alert – and
lucky – you'll spot the elusive dwarf and little bitterns, and purple and
lesser gallinules, secluded in the reedbeds.

African and lesser jacanas scurry across the lilypads, seeming almost to
walk on the water as they seek their food, small insects and aphids, on the
colourful waterlilies. The African jacana is an interesting bird in that it is
the male that incubates the eggs and raises the young once the female has
completed her only task – building the nest and laying the eggs. Thereafter
she departs in search of a new mate, leaving the male to take on all the
responsibilities of 'motherhood'. After the eggs hatch, the male carries the
shells away from the nest to dispose of them, presumably so as not to
attract predators. When out foraging for food, he often carries the young
chicks on his back, setting them down to hunt for themselves only when
he considers it safe. At any sign of danger, he squats and calls to the
chicks, who rush to his side and clamber into his breast feathers and
under his wings, where they take refuge until the danger is past.

The ugly and ungainly marabou stork, one of the largest of all flighted
birds, is widespread in the Delta, and can usually be found scavenging
alongside the vultures at the remains of kills and dead animals. In contrast,
the elegant and colourful yellowbilled storks, with their black and white
plumage tinged with a delicate pink, make a spectacular sight wherever
they gather in flocks that may number several hundred.

On the eastern side of the Delta the attractive wild date palms make way
for the coarse, towering ilala palms, landmark features on many islands
with their huge clusters of tennisball-size seeds, often numbering as many
as 2 000 to a tree. The seeds are favoured by elephants, which, during the
winter months when they move into the Delta in their thousands from the

ABOVE LEFT *The best way to
experience the peace and beauty of the
Okavango's waterways is in a dug-
out canoe.*

ABOVE *The clear waters of the
Okavango are home to many fish
species, and anglers come from around
the globe to practise their sport.*

drier lands to the east, can often be seen shaking these palms violently to get the fruit to fall to the ground.

Elephants also favour the fruit of the fabled marula tree, which can produce over a ton of fruit. This can be made into a potent alcoholic drink, and African folktales tell of animals becoming intoxicated after eating the fermenting fruits that have fallen to the ground.

The Okavango is a wildlife paradise, with year-round water, luxuriant grazing and a wide variety of indigenous trees providing both shade and nutritious browsing. Along with the adjoining Moremi Game Reserve and neighbouring Chobe National Park, it is home to vast multitudes of different game species – although numbers vary considerably depending on the time of year, and the state of the annual flood.

The flood is a result of torrential rainfall in the highlands of Angola – usually between November and March. These rains cause trickles to become torrents and streams to become raging rivers as the waters rush from the highlands and surge into the Cuito and Cubango rivers. The flow steadies and slows as it reaches the plains, and, while the effects are felt as early as March and April high in the Panhandle, the flood only begins to spill over and inundate the floodplains of the Okavango Delta much later in the year. Every year, for the residents of the Okavango, the questions are the same: How's the flood this year? Will it be a big one? Will it reach Maun (the capital village of the Delta)? In bad years, the water may not even get as far as the extreme southern reaches, and there are fears that Maun could run dry.

It is this flood that is the great provider of water for the Okavango Delta, as the rain which falls on the area immediately surrounding it merely soaks into the sand, and there is no runoff into its rivers and channels. The balance between the rainy season (November to March) and the flood season (June to August) is a useful one, for when the rains come to northern Botswana the game within the Delta can disperse into grazing areas too dry for them at other times of the year.

Okavango summers are therefore not ideal for game viewing, as not only are they hot, humid and often rainy and unpleasant, but most of the game animals have scattered and are difficult to find. With this knowledge in mind, many safari facilities close for the rainy season and only reopen at the end of summer when the game begins to filter back on to the floodplains of the Delta. For these reasons, the Delta cannot compare with Tanzania's Serengeti and Ngorongoro Crater or the parks of Kenya or South Africa as a purely game-viewing location. On the other hand, it does offer a real, unspoiled wilderness experience, with none of the over-crowding problems encountered in other popular game areas.

The Okavango's list of game is nevertheless a formidable one, although the further one ventures into the Delta proper, the wetlands, the fewer varieties one may expect to find. Baboons make up the largest single animal population, with as many as a quarter of a million scattered throughout the Okavango, living in troops of up to 100 individuals. The elusive sitatunga antelope attracts much attention, as many people who have lived in the Okavango for years have never seen one.

Another animal that favours the wetter areas is the red lechwe, an antelope which has today become endangered. For it, the Okavango Delta is paradise, its last stronghold. The lechwe is, in fact, one of the most common of all the antelope in the Delta, and is a specialized floodplain dweller, though somewhat less aquatic than the sitatunga.

In the many rivers and lagoons hippopotamus, crocodile and the giant Nile water monitor or leguaan are ever present, along with two types of otter, the Cape clawless and the spotted necked.

Of the large mammals, elephant and buffalo are the most plentiful – recent estimates based on aerial counts put the elephant population at as much as 55 000, with a growth rate of about six per cent annually, though only about 10 per cent of this number ever makes it into the Delta proper. One of the most memorable sights of all is that of a herd of elephants crossing one of the deeper lagoons, trunks raised periscope-like above the surface of the water. Sadly for the elephants, their numbers appear to be reaching dangerous levels and it is claimed that they are destroying their own and other animals' habitats to such an extent that man may have to step in to cull them.

Buffalo are present in their tens of thousands, and, at certain times of the year, one may experience the spectacular sight of herds numbering as many as a thousand trekking across the floodplains. These herds cover large distances as they move from one grazing ground to another, and often closer inspection of a pall of dust hanging in the distance will reveal a large herd on the move.

It is the cats though, that are always the most fascinating in any wilderness area, with the majestic lion holding most magic for the average person. Botswana has its fair share of lions, with the Kalahari lion reputed to be among the largest in Africa. Lions within the Okavango have adapted well to their watery surrounds, and move through water with little hesitation as they cross from island to island in search of prey.

The floodplains of the Okavango are ideal lion country, dotted as they are with well-wooded islands and shady termite mounds, which make excellent observation points for the tawny predators. The herds of buffalo, lechwe, impala, tsessebe and other prey species provide a ready supply of food. Okavango lions are, consequently, generally in fine condition – well fed and with coats less scarred than those of lions in the thorn country.

The spotted cats, leopard and cheetah, provide some of the biggest thrills for visitors to game country, and both occur throughout the Okavango. Leopard are primarily nocturnal hunters, secretive and elusive by day, and sightings are uncommon although these animals are by no means rare. Cheetah, by contrast, are adapted to hunt by day and are most active during the hours when their prey will be resting from the heat. However, they need open spaces in which to run down their victims, hunting by stealth combined with the animal kingdom's greatest speed – some 90 km/h. For this reason they are likely to be seen only on the larger open plains of the bigger islands, and in the areas surrounding the Delta, such as the Moremi Game Reserve and Chobe National Park.

Evening is a special time in the Okavango, strange and silent before the orchestra of the night strikes up. Sunset over one of the lagoons, palms silhouetted against the distant sky and the grunts and honks of awakening hippo echoing across the darkening waters, create a memory never to be forgotten. As darkness deepens and the creatures of the night awake, the Okavango takes on a new beauty. The lilting refrain of a nightjar competes with the strident whistle of a dikkop, penetrating a cacophony of windchime-like clinks, the mating calls of a thousand reedfrogs. Overhead, as a fire crackles at your feet, the tiny Scops owl whistles in the trees and the weird whoops of a distant hyena mingle with the high-pitched yips of a jackal on the prowl.

Suddenly comes that most entrancing sound of them all, the baritone roar of a lion on the hunt, trailing off with a succession of coughs, grunts and groans. The night goes still for a while, then the nervous whistle of a reedbuck breaks the silence as a golden moon edges over the horizon, its light reflecting on the shimmering waters below.

This is one of the magic moments in the wild, sitting silently beside a flickering fire, listening to the sounds of a million years as the mind wanders over the events of the day, and the promise of tomorrow. This is the Okavango, a fragile but enchanted wilderness, a glorious oasis in an ever-changing world.

BELOW *The camps and lodges of the Okavango are renowned for their 'haute bush cuisine', all the more impressive for being prepared in camp kitchens such as this one.*

BOTTOM *Okavango sunsets are often spectacular, and provide a fitting end to a day spent in this watery wonderland.*

LEFT *Sunrise over the Okavango presents the promise of another day of discovery and adventure.*

BELOW *A yellowbilled stork, plumage tinged with the delicate pink most noticeable in the breeding season, balances precariously atop a waterfig tree.*

RIGHT *Leopards often kill more than they can eat, and will store the surplus food in the branches of a tree, returning to finish the meal later. They have enormous strength and are able to climb trees with a load of as much as 100 kilograms.*

BELOW *Bat-eared foxes occur in the drier areas of the Okavango. Their large ears help them to detect insects – their primary food source – below the ground.*

OVERLEAF *When a herd is feeding, a few impala stand sentry around the perimeter. Should these sentries notice any potential danger, they alert the herd with a loud alarm snort; the impala then bunch together and, if the intruder is still some distance away, stand watching carefully.*

BELOW LEFT *An African jacana chick pecks at the blossom of a day-flowering lily. Note the long toes which enable it to walk across the lilypads.*

BELOW *Papyrus is one of the dominant plant species of the Okavango and occurs in abundance in the eastern sector along the Moanachira River and its offshoots. Dense and difficult to move through, it is an unpopular habitat for most larger species of game, and only the sitatunga, of the larger mammals, utilizes it both as a habitat and food source.*

The hippos' evil disposition and ill temper are widely respected in the Okavango, and local tribespeople in their mokoros *give them a wide berth whenever they are encountered.*

24

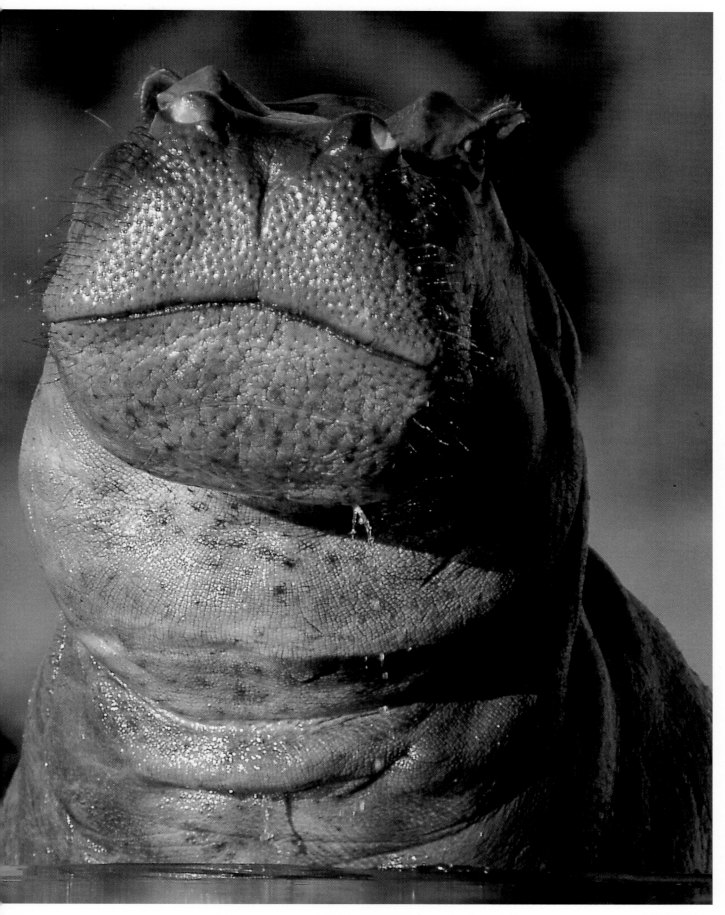

Semi-aquatic by nature, the red lechwe is generally found close to water and is common on the floodplains throughout the Delta. Although listed as an endangered species, lechwe are abundant in the Okavango wetlands.

LEFT *Elephant are perfectly at home in deep water and can sometimes be seen crossing large stretches during their annual migration.*

BELOW *Territorial defence between lechwe males mostly involves aggressive bluff, though occasionally serious wounds are inflicted.*

LEFT *Widely distributed throughout much of northern Botswana, Burchell's zebra are gregarious animals typically found in small family units comprising a stallion with several mares and their offspring.*

OVERLEAF *Primarily nocturnal, buffalo spend the heat of the day lying up under trees and bushes, only beginning to move soon after sunset, when they go down to water to drink.*

BELOW *Waterbuck bulls go through an elaborate nose-rubbing greeting ritual. Waterbuck are fiercely territorial and disputes between adult males often result in death.*

RIGHT *The snarling and neckbiting displayed by lions during copulation is a symbolic ritual rather than aggression. Courting couples like this pair move a short distance away from the rest of the pride, and coupling can take place as frequently as every 15 minutes over a period of several hours or longer.*

BELOW *Lion litters range from two to six cubs, which stay with their mother for 20 to 30 months, only hunting for themselves once they are between 18 and 24 months old.*

ABOVE *Grasping the prize in its talons, a fish eagle makes for its perch, probably in a prominent tree not far from the water's edge.*

FAR LEFT *Female ostriches are less attractive than their male counterparts; the latter sport splendid black plumage, which makes it easy to distinguish them from the dowdy grey females.*

LEFT *The plaintive cry of the fish eagle is one of the most evocative sounds of Africa. Particularly vociferous at dawn, these most attractive eagles, often singing in duet, produce a sound never to be forgotten.*

OVERLEAF *Statuesque and regal, the kudu is one of the most majestic of all the antelope. The spectacular long, spiral horns of the male kudu have made this species a favourite with hunters through the ages.*

BELOW *The marabou stork must rate as one of the ugliest of all birds – unpleasant in both looks and habits. Scavengers of carrion, marabous are frequently found at the remains of kills along with vultures, jackals and hyenas, as well as at rubbish heaps.*

BELOW RIGHT *Carmine bee-eaters typically nest in river banks and sand walls, but because of the flat nature of the Okavango's countryside, they tunnel down in suitable open sites, often as much as two metres deep. They are excellent fliers and perform spectacular acrobatic manoeuvres as they hunt flying insects on the wing.*

BELOW *A pied kingfisher watches patiently from its perch, ready to plummet headlong into the water when it sees a fish appear near the surface.*

BOTTOM *The day-flowering waterlilies can be seen in their thousands at certain times of the year, when they choke the shallower lagoons with a multi-hued carpet of delicate blossoms, and fill the air with their heady scent.*

OVERLEAF *No other animal can match a fully maned lion for sheer visual splendour. Okavango lions tend to be in better condition than their counterparts in the dry savannas of most of the rest of Africa.*

BELOW *Most of the biggest crocodiles in Botswana can be found in the Panhandle to the northwest of the Delta.*

RIGHT *A baboon quenches its thirst from a muddy hole. Baboons are the Okavango's most numerous large mammal, numbering about 250 000. They have a highly organized social hierarchy within troops, which may number as many as a hundred individuals.*

BELOW LEFT *Handsome and colourful, the saddlebill stork makes a stately figure as he stalks along the edge of a waterhole, or glides overhead.*

BELOW *Little bee-eaters are among the many beautiful varieties of birds found in the Delta, and are resident throughout the year.*

BOTTOM *The brilliant plumage of a carmine bee-eater provides a bright splash of colour in the Okavango countryside.*

BELOW *Elephants appear to be of the opinion that mud was made specially for them. They wallow in mud baths whenever possible, to protect themselves from the sun and relieve themselves of parasites, and seem to gain great pleasure from this activity.*

RIGHT *A cheetah keeps an attentive eye on a herd of impala grazing nearby. The fastest land animal on earth, the cheetah is both elegant and graceful, with a distinctly disdainful air. Once hunted extensively for their beautiful spotted coats, cheetah are today protected throughout most of their remaining range.*

ABOVE LEFT *A young impala ram adopts a jaunty attitude.*

ABOVE *Birds of prey, such as this juvenile chanting goshawk, abound throughout the Okavango and its surrounds.*

OVERLEAF *A young hyena relaxes in the early morning sun after a night on the prowl. The mournful call of the hyena, a series of long drawn-out whoops starting low down and rising up the scale, is one of the most memorable sounds of the African night.*

BELOW *The tiny tree-squirrel is one of the Okavango's smallest mammals, and a favourite with visitors to the Delta's many camps and lodges.*

BELOW *Giraffe are most vulnerable when drinking, and will normally only do so when others are in the vicinity to keep watch.*

ABOVE LEFT *An elephant bull shows his displeasure by making a mock charge, flapping his ears and trumpeting in annoyance. Generally peaceful animals, elephants can be aggressive and extremely dangerous when sick or injured. Threat displays usually involve raising the head and flapping the ears, kicking up dust with the forefeet and emitting a trumpeting*

scream . It may then mock charge,
swaying and shaking its massive head
as it does so. While this charge usually
breaks off once the desired effect is
achieved, it can develop into a serious
attack – with dire consequences.

ABOVE *Storm clouds gather as the late
afternoon sun casts a golden glow
over the landscape.*

LEFT *Giraffe give birth after a gestation period of 15 months, delivering their young in a standing position with hind legs bent to lessen the fall. The calf is up and able to walk, albeit unsteadily, within an hour of birth, but remains lying hidden in long grass for the first two to three weeks. Once strong enough to rejoin the group, the calf will be included in a nursery herd, which can number as many as a dozen or more infants and juveniles in the care of a few adult females.*

BELOW *Yellowbilled egrets flock to the protected nesting colony at Gadikwe Lagoon for the breeding season each year, joining the thousands of other birds that make the lagoon their home.*

ABOVE *Hippopotamuses are gregarious animals usually found in schools of between five and 15 but sometimes occurring in far larger concentrations when suitable stretches of water are at a premium. They are reputed to be responsible for more human deaths each year than any other animal.*

TOP *During the summer months, the spiky umbels of papyrus flowers produce thousands of seeds, which are dispersed by wind and water.*

ABOVE *Wings delicately etched against the sky, a pair of sacred ibis catch the late afternoon rays of sun as they fly homeward. Of the several varieties of ibis found in the Okavango, the sacred ibis is the most attractive.*

OVERLEAF *When rearing their young, lionesses often move onto remote, densely vegetated islands where they are relatively safe from attack .*

LEFT *A red-billed oxpecker probes a young buffalo bull's nostril for ticks and other parasites. Apart from the benefits gained by the de-ticking, buffalo find the oxpeckers useful as an early warning system, as the birds take to the air and chatter excitedly when approached by man or predators.*

ABOVE *The dainty impala is one of the most abundant of all antelope species in the game areas of southern Africa. They are generally found in herds of 20 to 30, but bigger groups can be seen in the drier months.*

OVERLEAF *The Okavango's rainy season comes in the summer months, with spectacular skies and dramatic thunderstorms that can dump several centimetres of rain on the parched land within a few hours.*

ABOVE *Sable antelope calves do not join the herd for the first two to three weeks of their lives, being unable to run with the adults to avoid danger. During this time they remain hidden in long grass or thick undergrowth, relying on an apparent lack of body odour to prevent detection by predators.*

LEFT *Although primarily nocturnal, the side-striped jackal may occasionally be seen in the early mornings, particularly in the cooler months when they may stay out to sun themselves before retiring to their burrows for the day.*

RIGHT *The hippo's ferocious teeth are used in displays of aggression and territorial fights. During the latter, serious, often fatal, wounds may be inflicted.*

OVERLEAF *A favourite with visitors to game reserves everywhere, the comical warthog occurs throughout the Okavango. Its familiar stiff-legged trot, tail erect, rarely fails to raise a laugh. The animal gets its name from the characteristic and conspicuous facial warts, of which the male has two pairs and the female one.*

RIGHT *The giraffe is one of Africa's most extraordinary animals, with an exceptionally long neck developed for browsing in the higher branches of trees. Surprisingly, though, a giraffe has only seven vertebrae in its neck, the same number as other mammals.*

BELOW *Elephants are dependent on water and drink about 160 litres a day. They will drink every day when water is available, but have been known to go several days without water when necessary. Being fussy animals, elephants prefer clean, sweet water and will often travel long distances to their favourite drinking places rather than utilize muddy water nearby.*

RIGHT AND BELOW RIGHT *The black egret is a fascinating bird that has developed a unique method of fishing for its prey. Stalking carefully through the water, it suddenly hunches forward and forms a canopy by bringing its wings forward and over its head. It then stirs the mud with its feet, probing with its bill for any prey.*

BELOW *Hippo are surprisingly fast both on land and in water, where they can either swim or walk along the bottom. They can remain underwater for five to seven minutes at a time, filling their lungs with a deep breath before submerging, and expelling it with a loud blast when resurfacing.*

Lion cubs are spotted when born, only losing their spots once they are several months old.

As the sun sets on another day in the Okavango, hippo begin to waken from their slumbers. Hippopotamus are nocturnal feeders, often walking 10 to 15 kilometres from the water to find food.